Dazzling Diamonds

Quilt Block of the Month™

Designs by Sandra L. Hatch and Sue Harvey

HOUSE of
WHITE
BIRCHES
PUBLISHERS
SINCE 1947

Introduction

This beautiful quilt was designed as a quilt-block-of-the-month project. There are nine original blocks. In month 10 add the sashing, in month 11 add the pieced borders and in month 12 you will complete the quilt. We have also given instructions to cut all the fabric and complete the quilt at once for those who won't be able to wait to complete the quilt one month at a time.

The Dazzling Diamonds sampler is a challenging design that yields beautiful results. Some of the blocks require more advanced piecing skills, but if you start with the easier blocks first, you should be prepared for the more difficult ones later on.

The instructions for cutting all the pieces for the quilt at one time are given, as well as instructions for cutting pieces for the blocks one at a time.

This makes the pattern suitable for use in a planned fabric arrangement as is shown in the sample or as a scrap quilt in colors of your own choosing.

Each pattern shows the most economical use of fabric, and the size needed of each fabric is listed to help you select scraps of the right size.

Samplers are always more work than other types of quilts because so many different blocks are used. But the results are always worth the effort. This sampler design is tied together by the sashing units, which are also repeated in some of the blocks. Each block design is an original.

You will enjoy making the blocks all your own by selecting fabric colors to suit your taste and decor. Whether you choose to make a coordinated quilt like the sample or a scrappy version, you should be proud of your finished quilt.

Meet the Designers

Sue Harvey

Sue Harvey and Sandra L. Hatch have been working together in the quilting world for many years. Sandra has been editing quilting magazines for more than 20 years. Sue has been working with her as the senior editor for *Quilter's World* since 2003. Before that time, they worked together on other quilting publications, including several previous books for House of White Birches.

Sandra comes from a sewing background with lots of experience and years of garment marking.

Sandra L. Hatch

She has also been a public-school sewing teacher. On the other hand, Sue has come to quiltmaking without sewing experience and the rules that go with it. She likes to say that she "doesn't know how to sew, only quilt." Their "right-way/wrong-way" styles have contributed to many lively designing sessions.

Because of their differing backgrounds, they have found that their book collaborations result in a wide variety of projects.

Cutting Instructions

You may choose to cut all your pieces at the same time or block by block. If cutting all at the same time, refer to the cutting instructions given here. If you prefer to cut block by block, refer to the cutting instructions and drawings given with individual blocks.

PROJECT NOTES

If you choose to purchase your fabrics for a planned arrangement to make the Dazzling Diamonds Sampler Quilt rather than cut pieces for blocks one at a time using scraps or other fabrics, we have included a list of materials needed along with cutting instructions for the entire quilt.

Cut the pieces listed before preparing and cutting template pieces.

PROJECT SPECIFICATIONS

Finished Quilt Size: 94" x 106"

MATERIALS

- ½ yard blue petal print
- ½ yard light blue tonal
- ¾ yard green marble
- ¾ yard navy print
- ⅞ yard dark purple print
- 1 yard light purple tonal
- 1⅛ yards yellow tonal
- 2¼ yards dark green print
- 3¾ yards cream tonal
- 4 yards floral
- 9½ yards backing fabric
- Batting 100" x 112"

SUPPLIES & TOOLS

- Cream and dark neutral threads
- Clear nylon monofilament or thread to match floral
- Quilting thread

- 2⅜ yards 12"-wide, lightweight double-stick fusible web
- Basic sewing tools and supplies

Cream Tonal Cutting

1. Cut six 1½" by fabric width strips; subcut strips into (56) 1½" G1 squares and (32) 4½" H1 rectangles.

2. Cut one 2⅜" by fabric width strip; subcut strip into eight 2" x 2" I1 squares and eight 2⅜" J1 squares. Cut each J1 square in half on one diagonal to make 16 J1 triangles.

3. Cut eight 2½" by fabric width strips; set aside four strips for Q1 and R1 border strips. Subcut the remaining strips into eight 2½" L1 squares, four 8½" N1 strips, four 10½" M1 strips and two 28½" O1 strips.

4. Cut (15) 2⅞" by fabric width strips; subcut strips into (206) 2⅞" squares; cut each square in half on one diagonal to make 412 B1 triangles.

5. Cut one 5¼" by fabric width strip; subcut strip into three 5¼" P1 squares and two 4¾" x 4¾" S1 squares. Cut all squares on both diagonals to make 12 P1 and eight S1 triangles.

6. Cut one 14⅞" by fabric width strip; subcut strip into two 14⅞" squares. Cut each square in half on one diagonal to make four T1 triangles.

Floral Cutting

1. Cut one 1½" by fabric width strip; subcut strip into (16) 1½" K1 squares.

2. Cut two 2½" by fabric width strips; subcut strips into eight each 3½" D1 and 4½" C1 rectangles.

3. Cut nine 3⅜" by fabric width strips; subcut strips into (105) 3⅜" A1 squares.

4. Cut nine 8½" by fabric width strips for U2 and V2 borders.

5. Cut one 3½" x 3½" E1 square.

6. Cut one 4⅛" x 4⅛" F1 square.

7. Cut one 18" by fabric width strip for Basket Medallion.

Light Purple Tonal Cutting

1. Cut eight 1½" by fabric width strips; set aside six strips for the pieced borders. Subcut remaining strips into two 13½" strips for Basket Medallion and (16) 1½" B2 squares.

2. Cut eight 2" x 2" D2 squares.

3. Cut one 2⅞" x 2⅞" square; cut in half on one diagonal to make two E2 triangles.

4. Cut one 3¼" x 3¼" square; cut on both diagonals to make four C2 triangles.

Green Marble Cutting

1. Cut one 1½" by fabric width strip; subcut strip into eight 1½" F2 squares.

2. Cut two 4⅞" by fabric width strips; subcut strips into (12) 4⅞" squares. Cut each square in half on one diagonal to make 24 H2 triangles.

Navy Print Cutting

1. Cut nine 1½" by fabric width strips; set aside six strips for pieced borders. Subcut one strip into three 13½" strips for Basket Medallion and two strips into (18) 4½" G2 rectangles.

2. Cut two 2½" x 21" strips for H/HR.

Dark Purple Print Cutting

1. Cut (10) 1½" by fabric width strips; set aside six

strips for pieced borders. Subcut remaining strips into eight 2½" K2 rectangles, two 13½" strips for Basket Medallion and (18) 4½" I2 rectangles.

2. Cut one 2⅜" by fabric width strip; subcut strip into eight 2⅜" squares. Cut each square in half on one diagonal to make 16 J2 triangles.

3. Cut two 2½" x 21" strips for H/HR.

Dark Green Print Cutting

1. Cut nine 1½" by fabric width strips; set aside seven strips for Q2 and R2 borders. Cut two each 10" L2 strips and 11" M2 strips from each of the remaining strips.

2. Cut (10) 2¼" by fabric width strips for binding.

3. Cut nine 2½" by fabric width strips; set aside eight strips for S2 and T2 borders. Subcut remaining strip into (16) 2½" N2 squares.

4. Cut two 3" x 3" squares; cut each square in half on one diagonal to make four O2 triangles.

5. Cut two 3⅜" x 3⅜" squares; cut each square in half on one diagonal to make four P2 triangles.

Yellow Tonal Cutting

1. Cut (15) 1½" by fabric width strips; set aside 12 strips for pieced borders. Subcut remaining strips into four 13½" strips for Basket Medallion and (24) 1½" X1 squares.

2. Cut two 3⅜" x 3⅜" squares; cut each square in half on one diagonal to make four Y1 triangles.

3. Cut two 4¼" x 4¼" squares; cut each square on both diagonals to make eight Z1 triangles.

Light Blue Tonal Cutting

1. Cut eight 1½" by fabric width strips; set aside six strips for pieced borders. Subcut remaining strips into two 13½" strips for Basket Medallion and (16) 1½" A2 squares.

Blue Petal Print Cutting

1. Cut one 3¼" x 3¼" square; cut on both diagonals to make four V1 triangles.

2. Cut one 2⅞" x 2⅞" square; cut in half on one diagonal to make two W1 triangles.

3. Cut four 2½" x 2½" U1 squares.

Templates

1. Prepare templates using pattern pieces given on pages 43–48. Cut as directed on each piece using remainder of fabrics. Label pieces and set aside in separate zipper bags to be used as needed for block and quilt piecing. **Note:** *Use the 2½" x 21" strips dark purple and navy prints to cut H and HR pieces referring to Figure 1 on page 36 (Completing the Center).*

2. Use an awl or large needle to punch a hole at the seam allowance corners on templates marked with dots to mark fabric pieces for set-in seams. When sewing these pieces, stop stitching at the marks. This allows the pieces to swivel when stitching set-in seams.

3. Place a ruler on the edge of template and use a rotary cutter to cut pieces. This saves time and eliminates cutting individual pieces. Be careful not to trim off the edge of your template. ▮

Hints

• If you plan to complete the blocks one at a time, set up a zipper bag for pieces for each block. Pin all pieces of the same letter together and label with a piece of masking tape to help make identification easy later on. Label the bag with the block name and place the printed instructions in the bag. This will help keep pieces from getting mixed up.

• It is important to press seams as indicated in the instructions. Be careful not to stretch pieces as you press because this will distort shapes making it harder to stitch perfect seams later on.

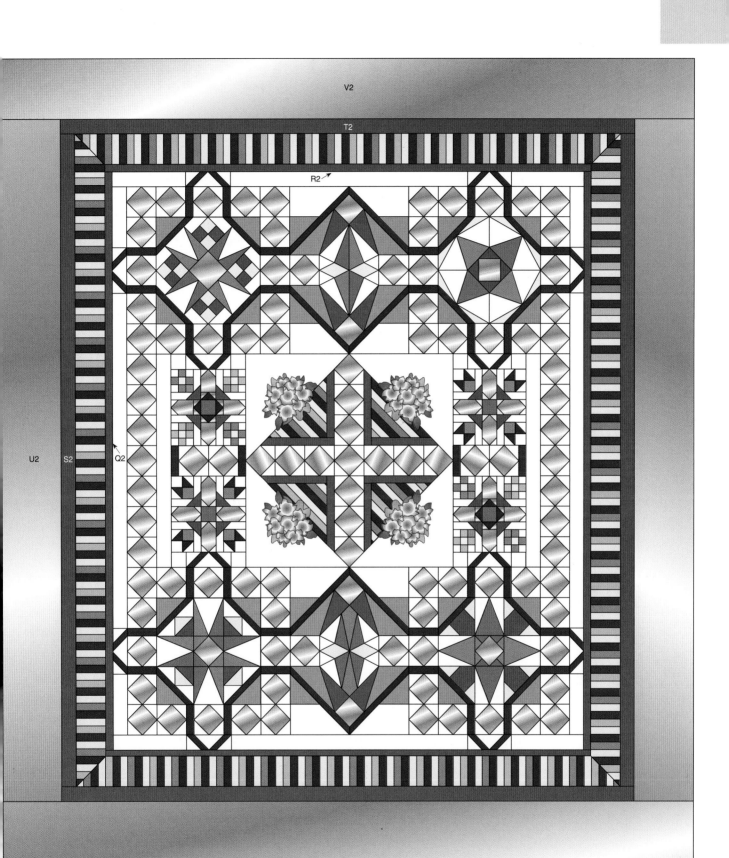

Dazzling Diamonds
Placement Diagram
94" x 106"

Tulips in the Corners

Kick-start your quilt with two rotary-cut and quick-pieced blocks.

PROJECT SPECIFICATIONS
Block Size: 10" x 10"
Number of Blocks: 2

FABRICS NEEDED
- 6" x 21" strip floral
- 6" by fabric width strip cream tonal
- 3" x 21" strip dark green print
- 3" x 6" rectangle blue petal print
- 3" x 20" strip dark purple print
- 3" x 17" strip light purple tonal
- 4" x 13" strip yellow tonal

Tulips in the Corners
10" x 10" Block

Cutting Instructions

Note: *If you have previously cut all the pieces for the quilt, disregard these cutting instructions and go directly to Piecing the Blocks.*

1. Refer to Cutting Chart on page 10 for cutting all pieces for best use of fabric.

2. Cut two 2½" x 2½" U1 squares blue petal print.

3. Cut (16) 1½" x 1½" X1 squares yellow tonal.

4. Cut eight 2½" x 4½" C1 rectangles floral.

5. Cut eight 2" x 2" D2 squares light purple tonal.

6. Cut eight 2½" x 2½" N2 squares dark green print.

7. Cut (16) 1½" x 4½" H1 rectangles cream tonal.

8. Cut (16) 1½" x 1½" G1 squares cream tonal.

9. Cut eight 2⅜" x 2⅜" squares cream tonal; cut each square in half on one diagonal to make 16 J1 triangles.

10. Cut eight 2" x 2" I1 squares cream tonal.

11. Cut eight 2⅜" x 2⅜" squares dark purple print; cut each square in half on one diagonal to make 16 J2 triangles.

Piecing the Blocks

1. Draw a diagonal line from corner to corner on the wrong side of each X1, N2 and G1 square.

2. Place X1 on one corner of C1 as shown in Figure 1; stitch on the marked line, trim seam allowance to ¼" and press X1 to the right side, again referring to Figure 1.

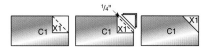

Figure 1

3. Repeat on the adjacent corner of C1 as shown in Figure 2.

Figure 2

4. Repeat steps 2 and 3 with G1 squares on the remaining corners of C1 to complete one C1 unit as shown in Figure 3. Repeat to make eight C1 units.

Figure 3

5. Sew J1 to J2 along the diagonal as shown in Figure 4; press seam toward J2. Repeat to make 16 J1-J2 units.

Figure 4

6. Referring to Figure 5, sew a J1-J2 unit to I1; repeat for eight J1-J2-I1 units. Repeat with J1-J2 and D2 to make eight J1-J2-D2 units. Press seams toward I1 and D2.

Figure 5

7. Join one each J1-J2-I1 and J1-J2-D2 units to complete a corner unit, again referring to Figure 5; repeat for eight pieced units. Press seams in one direction.

8. Sew H1 to two adjacent sides of each pieced unit, aligning one end of H1 with the J1 end of the pieced unit as shown in Figure 6; press seams toward H1.

Figure 6

9. Place N2 right sides together on the H1 corner of one pieced unit as shown in Figure 7; stitch on the marked line, trim seam allowance to ¼" and press N2 to the right side to complete one corner unit, again referring to Figure 7. Repeat to make eight corner units.

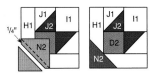

Figure 7

10. Sew a C1 unit to opposite sides of U1 with the X1 corners against U1 to complete a block center row referring to the block drawing for positioning of pieces; press seams toward U1. Repeat to make two center rows.

11. Sew a C1 unit between two corner units to complete a side row referring to the block drawing for positioning of pieces; press seams toward the corner units. Repeat to make four side rows.

12. Sew a center row between two side rows to complete one block; press seams toward the center row. Repeat to complete two blocks. ■

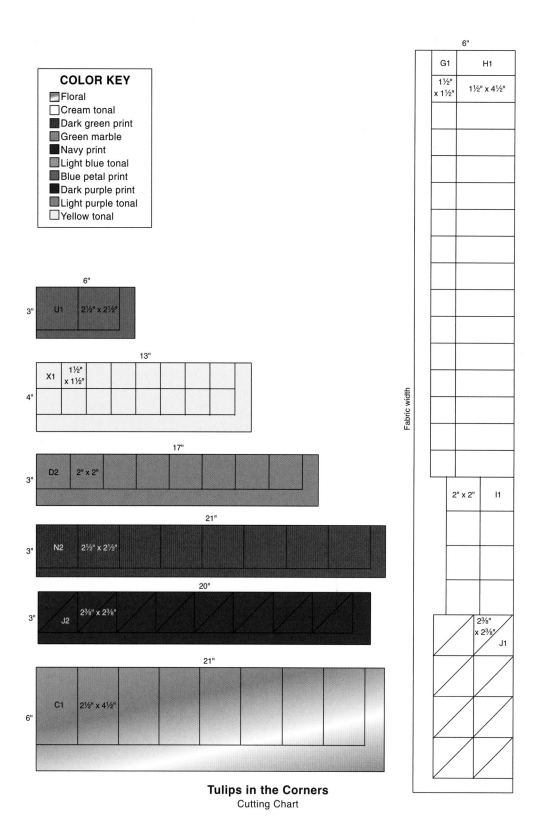

COLOR KEY
- Floral
- Cream tonal
- Dark green print
- Green marble
- Navy print
- Light blue tonal
- Blue petal print
- Dark purple print
- Light purple tonal
- Yellow tonal

Tulips in the Corners
Cutting Chart

Nine-Patch Flowers

Simple Nine-Patch units create pretty flower corners on your second set of blocks.

PROJECT SPECIFICATIONS
Block Size: 10" x 10"
Number of Blocks: 2

FABRICS NEEDED
- 6" x 25" rectangle floral
- 13" x 17" rectangle cream tonal
- 3" x 21" strip dark green print
- 4" x 7" rectangle green marble
- 7" square light blue tonal
- 3" x 6" rectangle blue petal print
- 4" x 11" rectangle dark purple print
- 7" square light purple tonal
- 4" x 7" rectangle yellow tonal

Cutting Instructions
Note: If you have previously cut all the pieces for the quilt, disregard these cutting instructions and go directly to Piecing the Blocks.

1. Refer to Cutting Chart on page 13 for cutting all pieces for best use of fabric.

2. Cut eight 1½" x 2½" K2 rectangles dark purple print.

3. Cut eight 2½" x 3½" D1 rectangles and (16) 1½" x 1½" K1 squares floral.

4. Cut eight 2½" x 2½" N2 squares dark green print.

5. Cut (16) 1½" x 4½" H1 rectangles and (40) 1½" x 1½" G1 squares cream tonal.

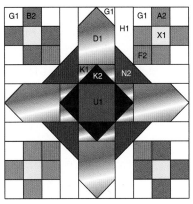

Nine-Patch Flowers
10" x 10" Block

6. Cut (16) 1½" x 1½" A2 squares light blue tonal.

7. Cut eight 1½" x 1½" F2 squares green marble.

8. Cut eight 1½" x 1½" X1 squares yellow tonal.

9. Cut (16) 1½" x 1½" B2 squares light purple tonal.

10. Cut two 2½" U1 squares blue petal print.

Piecing the Blocks
1. Draw a diagonal line from corner to corner on the wrong side of each K1, N2 and 16 G1 squares.

2. Place K1 on one end of K2 as shown in Figure 1; stitch on the marked line, trim seam allowance to ¼" and press K1 to the right side, again referring to Figure 1.

Figure 1

3. Repeat on the remaining end of K2 to complete one K2-K1 unit as shown in Figure 2. Repeat to make eight K2-K1 units.

Figure 2

4. Place G1 on one corner of D1, stitch, trim seam allowance and press G1 to the right side as shown in Figure 3. Repeat on the adjacent corner of D1 to complete one D1-G1 unit, again referring to Figure 3. Repeat to make eight D1-G1 units.

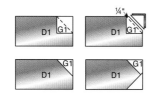

Figure 3

5. Arrange G1, A2, F2 and X1 squares in three rows of three squares each as shown in Figure 4.

Figure 4

6. Join squares in rows; press seams toward A2. Join rows to complete one A2 unit; press seams in one direction. Repeat to make four A2 units.

7. Repeat steps 5 and 6 to make four B2 units as shown in Figure 5.

Figure 5

8. Sew H1 to two adjacent sides of each A2 and B2 unit, aligning one end of H1 with the G1 end of the unit as shown in Figure 6; press seams toward H1.

Figure 6

9. Place N2 right sides together on the H1 corner of one pieced unit as shown in Figure 7; stitch on the marked line, trim seam allowance to ¼" and press N2 to the right side to complete one corner unit, again referring to Figure 7. Repeat to make four each A2 and B2 corner units.

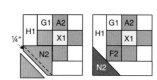

Figure 7   **Figure 8**

10. Sew a K2-K1 unit to the D1 end of each D1-G1 unit to complete eight side units as shown in Figure 8; press seams toward D1-G1.

11. Sew a side unit to opposite sides of U1 to complete a block center row referring to the block drawing for positioning of pieces; press seams toward U1. Repeat to make two center rows.

12. Sew a side unit between one each A2 and B2 corner units to make a side row referring to the block drawing for positioning of pieces; press seams toward the corner units. Repeat to make four side rows.

13. Sew a center row between two side rows to complete one block; press seams toward the center row. Repeat to complete two blocks. ■

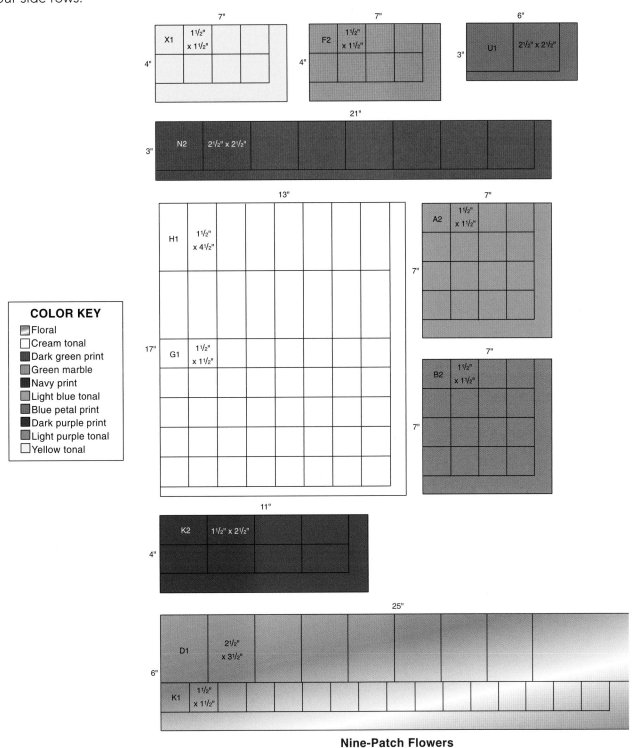

COLOR KEY
- Floral
- Cream tonal
- Dark green print
- Green marble
- Navy print
- Light blue tonal
- Blue petal print
- Dark purple print
- Light purple tonal
- Yellow tonal

Nine-Patch Flowers
Cutting Chart

Tumbling Stars

Sharpen your piecing skills with the set-in pieces of the first star block.

PROJECT SPECIFICATIONS
Block Size: 14" x 14"
Number of Blocks: 1

FABRICS NEEDED
- 5" square floral
- 6" x 28" strip cream tonal
- 4" x 9" strip navy print
- 6" x 9" rectangle blue petal print
- 4" x 9" rectangle dark purple print
- 6" x 9" rectangle light purple tonal
- 4" x 17" strip yellow tonal
- 6" x 11" rectangle green marble
- 4" x 7" rectangle dark green print

Cutting Instructions
Note: If you have previously cut all the pieces for the quilt, disregard these cutting instructions and go directly to Piecing the Block.

1. Prepare templates for B, C, I and J pieces.

2. Refer to Cutting Chart on page 16 for cutting all pieces listed on templates for Tumbling Star and below for best use of fabric. Mark a dot at the seam allowance corners on the wrong side of each B, C, CR, J and JR piece as marked on patterns.

3. Cut one 3½" x 3½" E1 square floral.

4. Cut two 3" x 3" dark green print O2 squares; cut each square in half on one diagonal to make four O2 triangles.

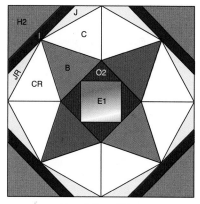

Tumbling Star
14" x 14" Block

5. Cut two 4⅞" x 4⅞" squares green marble; cut each square in half on one diagonal to make four H2 triangles.

Piecing the Block
1. Sew O2 to each side of E1 to make an E1-O2 unit as shown in Figure 1; press seams toward O2.

Figure 1

2. Sew C and CR to two sides of B to make a B-C unit as shown in Figure 2, beginning and ending stitching at the marked corner dots; press seams toward B. Repeat to make two blue petal and two light purple B-C units.

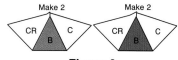

Figure 2

3. Sew a B-C unit to each side of the E1-O2 unit, beginning and ending stitching at the marked corner dot on the B pieces and alternating colors as shown in Figure 3.

Figure 3

4. Stitch the seam between the C and CR pieces, beginning at the marked corner dot as shown in Figure 4 to complete the center unit; press seam of B-C units toward E1-O2 and the seam between C and CR open.

Figure 4

5. Sew a J piece to each C piece and a JR piece to each CR piece around the center unit as shown in Figure 5; press seams toward C or CR.

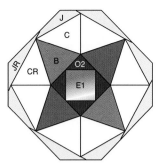

Figure 5

6. Sew a navy or dark purple I piece to each H2 triangle as shown in Figure 6; press seam toward H2.

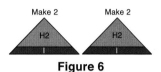

Figure 6

7. Sew an H2-I unit to each J/JR side of the center unit referring to the block drawing for positioning; press seams toward H2-I to complete the Tumbling Star block. ■

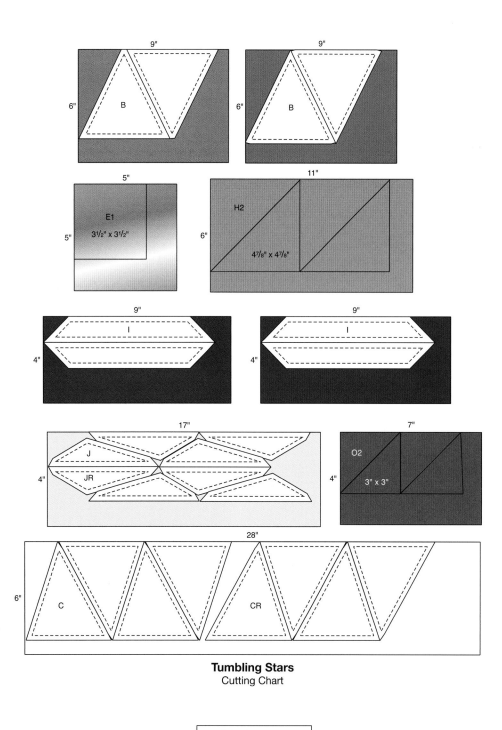

Tumbling Stars
Cutting Chart

COLOR KEY

- Floral
- Cream tonal
- Dark green print
- Green marble
- Navy print
- Light blue tonal
- Blue petal print
- Dark purple print
- Light purple tonal
- Yellow tonal

Elongated Star

Be careful with your seam allowance to create nice sharp points on this star.

PROJECT SPECIFICATIONS
Block Size: 14" x 14"
Number of Blocks: 1

FABRICS NEEDED
- 4" square floral
- 11" x 13" rectangle cream tonal
- 4" x 9" strip navy print
- 7" x 10" rectangle blue petal print
- 4" x 9" strip dark purple print
- 7" x 10" rectangle light purple tonal
- 4" x 8" rectangle yellow tonal
- 6" x 11" rectangle green marble
- 4" x 8" rectangle dark green print

Cutting Instructions
Note: *If you have previously cut all the pieces for the quilt, disregard these cutting instructions and go directly to Piecing the Block.*

1. Prepare templates for D, E and I pieces.

2. Refer to Cutting Chart on page 19 for cutting all pieces listed on templates for Elongated Star and below for best use of fabric.

3. Cut one 3⅜" x 3⅜" A1 square floral.

4. Cut one 2⅞" x 2⅞" square each light purple tonal (E2) and blue petal print (W1); cut each square in half on one diagonal to make two each E2 and W1 triangles.

5. Cut two 4¾" x 4¾" squares cream tonal; cut each square on both diagonals to make eight S1 triangles.

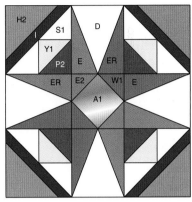

Elongated Star
14" x 14" Block

6. Cut two 3⅜" x 3⅜" squares dark green print; cut each square in half on one diagonal to make four P2 triangles.

7. Cut two 3⅜" x 3⅜" squares yellow tonal; cut each square in half on one diagonal to make four Y1 triangles.

8. Cut two 4⅞" x 4⅞" squares green marble; cut each square in half on one diagonal to make four H2 triangles.

Piecing the Block
1. Sew E2 to opposite sides of A1 as shown in Figure 1; press seams toward E2. Repeat with W1 on the remaining sides of A1, again referring to Figure 1; press seams toward W1.

Figure 1

2. Sew a light purple tonal E and a blue petal print ER to D to complete a side unit as shown in

Figure 2; press seams toward E and ER. Repeat to make four side units, again referring to Figure 2.

Make 2   Make 2

Figure 2

3. Sew P2 to Y1 along the diagonal; press seam toward P2. Repeat to make four P2-Y1 units.

4. Sew S1 to each Y1 side of the P2-Y1 units as shown in Figure 3; press seams toward S1.

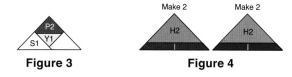

Make 2   Make 2

Figure 3   **Figure 4**

5. Sew I to H2 as shown in Figure 4; press seam toward H2. Repeat to make four H2-I units, again referring to Figure 4.

6. Sew an H2-I unit to the S1 side of each S1-Y1-P2 unit to make a corner unit as shown in

Figure 5; press seams toward H2-I. Repeat for four corner units.

Figure 5

7. Sew the A-E2-W1 unit between two side units to make the block center row referring to the block drawing for positioning of units; press seams toward A-E2-W1.

8. Sew a side unit between two corner units to make a side row referring to the block drawing for positioning of units; press seams toward corner units. Repeat to make two side rows.

9. Sew the center row between the side rows to complete the block referring to the block drawing for positioning of rows; press seams toward the center row. ∎

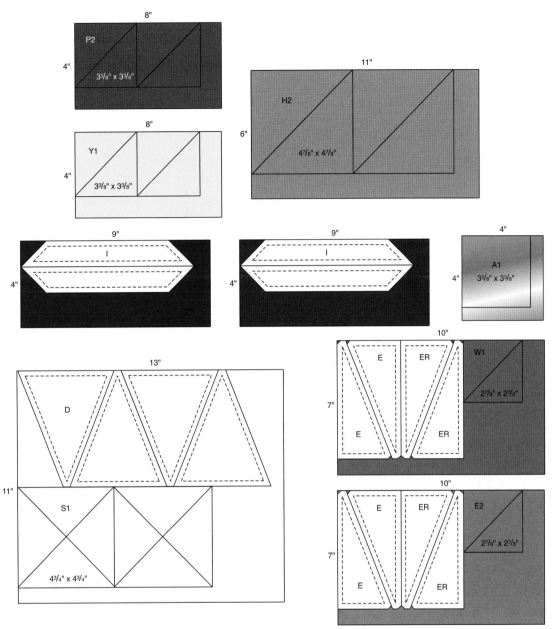

Elongated Star
Cutting Chart

COLOR KEY

- Floral
- Cream tonal
- Dark green print
- Green marble
- Navy print
- Light blue tonal
- Blue petal print
- Dark purple print
- Light purple tonal
- Yellow tonal

Starry Hearts

Turn the star-point units from the Elongated Star to make the heart shapes in this block.

PROJECT SPECIFICATIONS
Block Size: 14" x 14"
Number of Blocks: 1

FABRICS NEEDED
- 4" square floral
- 7" x 14" rectangle cream tonal
- 4" x 9" rectangle navy print
- 7" x 12" rectangle blue petal print
- 4" x 9" rectangle dark purple print
- 7" x 12" rectangle light purple tonal
- 5" x 10" rectangle yellow tonal
- 6" x 11" rectangle green marble
- 5" x 15" rectangle dark green print

Cutting Instructions
Note: If you have previously cut all the pieces for the quilt, disregard these cutting instructions and go directly to Piecing the Block.

1. Prepare templates for D, E, G and I pieces.

2. Refer to Cutting Chart on page 22 for cutting all pieces listed on templates for Starry Hearts and below for best use of fabric.

3. Cut one 3⅜" x 3⅜" A1 square floral.

4. Cut one 3¼" x 3¼" square each light purple tonal (C2) and blue petal print (V1); cut each square on both diagonals to make four each C2 and V1 triangles.

5. Cut two 4¼" x 4¼" squares yellow tonal; cut each square on both diagonals to make eight Z1 triangles.

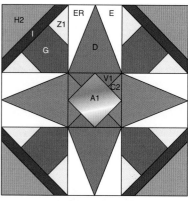

Starry Hearts
14" x 14" Block

6. Cut two 4⅞" x 4⅞" squares green marble; cut each square in half on one diagonal to make four H2 triangles.

Piecing the Block
1. Sew V1 to C2 as shown in Figure 1; press seam toward V1. Repeat for four V1-C2 units.

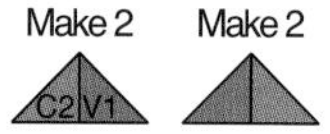

Make 2   Make 2

Figure 1

2. Sew a V1-C2 unit to each side of A1 as shown in Figure 2; press seams toward A1.

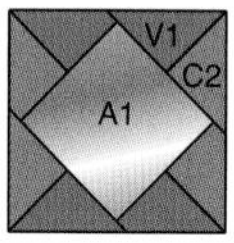

Figure 2

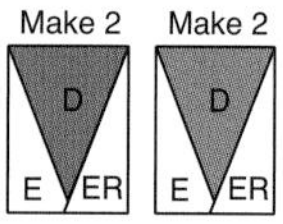

Make 2   Make 2

Figure 3

3. Sew E and ER to D to make a side unit as shown in Figure 3; press seams toward E. Repeat to make four side units.

4. Sew Z1 to opposite sides of G as shown in Figure 4; press seams toward G. Repeat to make four Z1-G units.

Figure 4

5. Sew I to H2 as shown in Figure 5; press seams toward H2. Repeat to make four H2-I units.

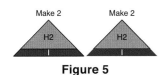

Make 2   Make 2

Figure 5   **Figure 6**

6. Sew an H2-I unit to a Z1-G unit to complete a corner unit as shown in Figure 6; press seam

toward H2-I. Repeat to make four corner units.

7. Sew the A1-V1-C2 unit between two light purple side units to make the block center row referring to the block drawing for positioning of units; press seams toward A1-V1-C2.

8. Sew a blue petal side unit between two corner units to make a side row referring to the block drawing for positioning of units; press seams toward the corner units. Repeat to make two side rows.

9. Sew the center row between the two side rows to complete the block referring to the block drawing for positioning of rows; press seams toward the side rows. ■

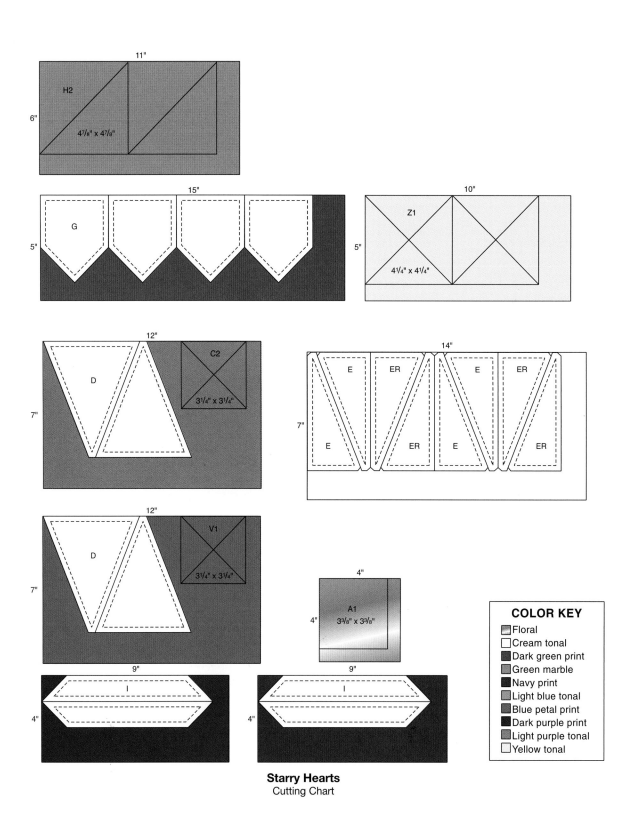

Starry Hearts
Cutting Chart

COLOR KEY
- Floral
- Cream tonal
- Dark green print
- Green marble
- Navy print
- Light blue tonal
- Blue petal print
- Dark purple print
- Light purple tonal
- Yellow tonal

Four-Patch Star

Four-Patch units nestle between the star points in the last of the 14" blocks.

PROJECT SPECIFICATIONS
Block Size: 14" x 14"
Number of Blocks: 1

FABRICS NEEDED
- 5" square floral
- 7" x 21" rectangle cream tonal
- 4" x 9" strip navy print
- 6" x 7" rectangle blue petal print
- 4" x 9" strip dark purple print
- 6" x 7" rectangle light purple tonal
- 3" x 18" strip yellow tonal
- 6" x 11" rectangle green marble
- 3" x 18" strip dark green print

Cutting Instructions
Note: If you have previously cut all the pieces for the quilt, disregard these cutting instructions and go directly to Piecing the Block.

1. Prepare templates for I, K, L, M and P pieces.

2. Refer to Cutting Chart on page 25 for cutting all pieces listed on templates for Four-Patch Star and below for best use of fabric.

3. Cut one 4⅛" x 4⅛" F1 square floral.

4. Cut two 4⅞" x 4⅞" squares green marble; cut each square in half on one diagonal to make four H2 triangles.

Piecing the Block
1. Sew M and MR to L as shown in Figure 1; press

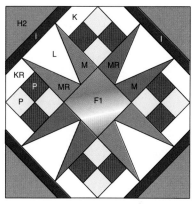

Four-Patch Star
14" x 14" Block

seams toward M and MR. Repeat to make four L-M units, again referring to Figure 1.

Figure 1

2. Join two each yellow tonal and dark green print P squares to make a Four-Patch unit as shown in Figure 2; press seams toward dark green print. Repeat to make four units.

Figure 2

Figure 3

3. Sew K and KR to two adjacent sides of each Four-Patch unit to make a corner unit as shown in Figure 3; press seams toward K and KR.

4. Sew the F1 square between two blue L-M units to make the center row as shown in Figure 4; press seams toward F1.

Figure 4

5. Sew a light purple L-M unit between two corner units to make a side row as shown in Figure 5; press seams toward the corner units. Repeat to make two side rows.

Figure 5

6. Sew the center row between the two side rows to complete the block center referring to the block drawing for positioning of rows; press seams toward the center row.

7. Sew I to H2 as shown in Figure 6; press seam toward H2. Repeat to make four H2-I units, again referring to Figure 6.

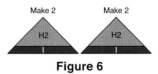

Figure 6

8. Sew an H2-I unit to each L side of the block center to complete the block referring to the block drawing for positioning of units; press seams toward H2-I. ∎

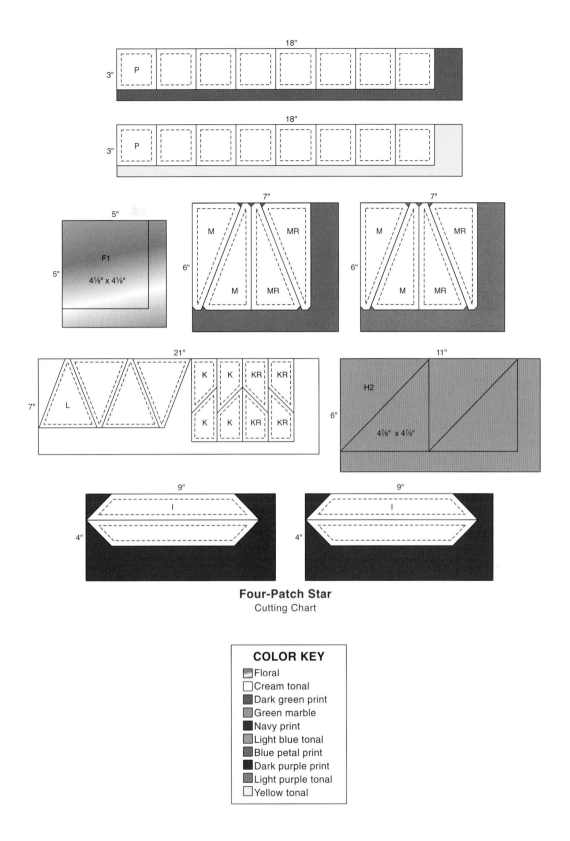

Four-Patch Star
Cutting Chart

COLOR KEY
- Floral
- Cream tonal
- Dark green print
- Green marble
- Navy print
- Light blue tonal
- Blue petal print
- Dark purple print
- Light purple tonal
- Yellow tonal

Star Reflections

Congratulations! You've worked your way to the more difficult rectangular blocks. Use an accurate ¼" seam allowance and mark the corners of your pieces as directed, and you'll have no problem with this one.

PROJECT SPECIFICATIONS
Block Size: 16" x 22"
Number of Blocks: 1

FABRICS NEEDED
- 8" square floral
- 13" x 21" rectangle cream tonal
- 4" x 14" strip navy print
- 4" x 9" strip blue petal print
- 4" x 14" strip dark purple print
- 4" x 9" strip light purple tonal
- 6" square yellow tonal
- 14" square green marble
- 8" x 9" rectangle dark green print

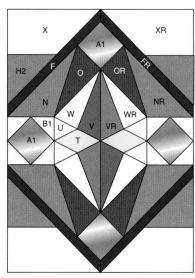

Star Reflections
16" x 22" Block

Cutting Instructions
Note: If you have previously cut all the pieces for the quilt, disregard these cutting instructions and go directly to Piecing the Block.

1. Prepare templates for F, N, O, T, U, V, W and X pieces.

2. Refer to Cutting Chart on page 28 for cutting all pieces listed on templates for Star Reflections and below for best use of fabric.

3. Cut four 3⅜" x 3⅜" A1 squares floral.

4. Cut four 2⅞" x 2⅞" squares cream tonal; cut each square in half on one diagonal to make eight B1 triangles.

5. Cut two 4⅞" x 4⅞" squares green marble; cut each square in half on one diagonal to make four H2 triangles.

Piecing the Block

1. Sew V to W as shown in Figure 1; press seam toward W. Repeat for two each V-W and VR-WR units, again referring to Figure 1.

Figure 1

Figure 2

2. Sew U to two adjacent edges of T as shown in Figure 2; press seams toward T. Repeat for two T-U units.

3. Sew V-W to one edge of T-U and VR-WR to the other edge of T-U as shown in Figure 3; press seams in one direction. Repeat for two pieced units.

Figure 3   **Figure 4**

4. Join the pieced units as shown in Figure 4; press seam open.

5. Sew O to opposite W edges of the pieced unit as shown in Figure 5; press seams toward O.

Figure 6

Figure 5

6. Sew A1 to the square end of each OR piece as shown in Figure 6; press seams toward OR.

7. Sew an A1-OR unit to the WR edges of the pieced unit to complete the center unit as shown in Figure 7; press seams toward A1-OR.

Figure 8

Figure 7

8. Sew B1 to each side of A1 as shown in Figure 8; press seams toward B1. Repeat for two A1-B1 units.

9. Sew N and NR to opposite sides of each A1-B1 unit as shown in Figure 9, stopping stitching at the marked corner dot on the N and NR pieces; press seams toward N and NR.

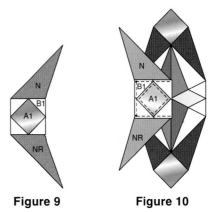

Figure 9   **Figure 10**

10. Sew the A1-B1 edge of the A1-B1-N units to the T-U edges of the pieced center unit, beginning and ending stitching at the marked corner dots on the N and NR pieces as shown in Figure 10.

11. Sew the N and NR edges to the O and OR edges, beginning stitching at the marked corner dots on the N and NR pieces as shown in Figure 11; press seams toward A1-B1-N units.

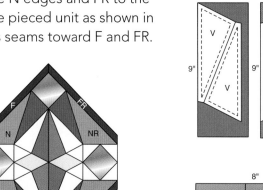

Figure 11

12. Sew F to the N edges and FR to the NR edges of the pieced unit as shown in Figure 12; press seams toward F and FR.

Figure 12

13. Sew H2 to X as shown in Figure 13; press seam toward H2. Repeat to make two each H2-X and H2-XR units, again referring to Figure 13.

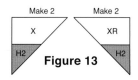

Figure 13

14. Sew the H2-X units to the F sides and the H2-XR units to the FR sides of the pieced unit to complete the block referring to the block drawing for positioning of units; press seams toward H2-X and H2-XR units. ∎

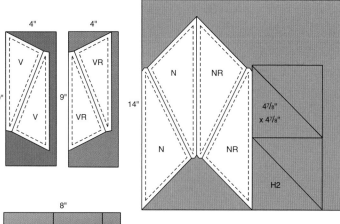

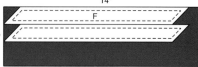

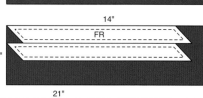

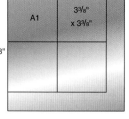

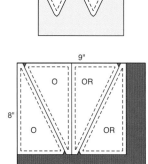

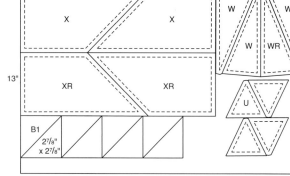

Star Reflections
Cutting Chart

COLOR KEY
- Floral
- Cream tonal
- Dark green print
- Green marble
- Navy print
- Light blue tonal
- Blue petal print
- Dark purple print
- Light purple tonal
- Yellow tonal

Basket Medallion

Use your imagination to create the appliquéd bouquets that fill each strip-pieced basket. Hand- or machine-appliqué as many or as few fussy-cut flowers from the floral fabric to make this block uniquely your own.

PROJECT NOTE
Try a variegated or metallic thread to add another dimension to the appliquéd flowers.

PROJECT SPECIFICATIONS
Block Size: 28" x 28"
Number of Blocks: 1

FABRICS NEEDED
- 1½" x 42" strip navy print
- 4" x 15" strip light blue tonal
- 4" x 15" strip dark purple print
- 4" x 15" strip light purple tonal
- ⅛ yard yellow tonal
- ⅛ yard dark green print
- ⅔ yard cream tonal
- 1 yard floral

MATERIALS FOR MACHINE APPLIQUÉ
- 2⅜ yards 12"-wide lightweight double-stick fusible web
- Clear nylon monofilament

Cutting Instructions
Note: If you have previously cut all the pieces for the quilt, disregard these cutting instructions and go directly to Piecing the Block.

1. Cut two 1½" x 13½" strips each light blue tonal, light purple tonal and dark purple print.

2. Cut three 1½" x 13½" navy print strips.

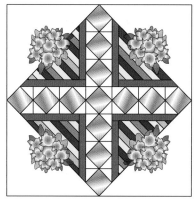

Basket Medallion
28" x 28" Block

3. Cut two 1½" by fabric width strips yellow tonal; subcut strips into four 13½" strips.

4. Cut two 3⅜" by fabric width strips floral; subcut strips into (13) 3⅜" A1 squares.

5. Cut two 2⅞" by fabric width strips cream tonal; subcut strips into (22) 2⅞" squares. Cut each square in half on one diagonal to make 44 B1 triangles.

6. Cut two 14⅞" x 14⅞" squares cream tonal; cut each square in half on one diagonal to make four T1 triangles.

7. Cut two 1½" by fabric width strips dark green print; subcut each strip into two 10" L2 strips and two 11" M2 strips.

8. Cut one 18" by fabric width strip floral for basket appliqué.

Piecing the Block

1. Join the 13½"-long strips to make a 13½" pieced square referring to Figure 1 for order of stitching; press seams in one direction.

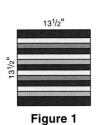

Figure 1

Trim to 12⅝" x 12⅝"

Figure 2

2. Trim the pieced square to make a 12⅝" x 12⅝" square as shown in Figure 2.

3. Cut the square on both diagonals to make four pieced triangles as shown in Figure 3.

Figure 3

Figure 4

4. Sew an L2 strip to one short side and an M2 strip to the adjacent short side of each pieced triangle as shown in Figure 4; press seams toward L2 and M2.

5. Trim the ends of the L2 and M2 strips even with the long edge of the pieced triangles to complete the basket units as shown in Figure 5.

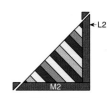

Figure 5

6. Sew a B1 triangle to each side of A1 as shown in Figure 6; press seams toward B1. Repeat to make nine A1-B1 units.

Make 9

Make 4

Figure 6   **Figure 7**

7. Sew a B1 triangle to two adjacent sides of A1 as shown in Figure 7; press seams toward B1. Repeat to make four end units.

8. Join two A1-B1 units with one end unit to make a strip as shown in Figure 8; press seams open between units. Repeat for two strips.

Make 2

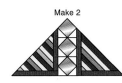

Make 2

Figure 8   **Figure 9**

9. Join two basket units with one strip referring to Figure 9 for positioning of basket units; press seams toward basket units. Repeat.

10. Join five A1-B1 units with two end units to make a strip as shown in Figure 10; press seams open between units.

Figure 10

11. Join the basket sections with the pieced strip referring to Figure 11 for positioning of basket sections; press seams toward basket sections.

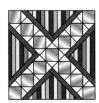

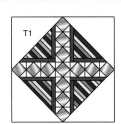

Figure 11   **Figure 12**

12. Sew a T1 triangle to each edge of the pieced unit as shown in Figure 12; press seams toward T1.

Adding the Appliqué

1. For hand appliqué, choose flowers and flower clusters from the ½-yard floral piece and cut out adding a ⅛"–¼" seam allowance around each piece.

2. Arrange the flowers on each T1 triangle as desired, overlapping inside seam allowance edges and leaving at least ½" clear along outer edges of T1.

3. When satisfied with positioning, pin to hold.

4. Hand-stitch in place with matching thread to complete the block, turning seam allowances under on exposed edges as you stitch.

5. For machine appliqué, cut one 12" x 42" piece and one 6" x 42" piece of fusible web; remove paper liner.

6. Lightly bond to cover wrong side of the 18" by fabric width strip floral.

7. Choose flowers and flower clusters and cut out on the motif lines; remove remaining paper.

8. Arrange the flowers on each T1 triangle as desired, overlapping edges and leaving at least ½" clear along outer edges of T1. ***Note:*** *You may bond the remaining fusible web on sections of the remaining floral if more flowers are needed.*

9. When satisfied with positioning, fuse pieces in place.

10. Using clear nylon monofilament and a straight or zigzag stitch, machine-stitch pieces in place along all edges to complete the block. ■

COLOR KEY
☐ Floral
☐ Cream tonal
■ Dark green print
▨ Green marble
■ Navy print
☐ Light blue tonal
▨ Blue petal print
■ Dark purple print
▨ Light purple tonal
☐ Yellow tonal

Starry Garden

The center points in this one are a bit tricky. Pay close attention to the stitching and pressing instructions to complete a block that will make you proud.

PROJECT SPECIFICATIONS
Block Size: 16" x 22"
Number of Blocks: 1

FABRICS NEEDED
- 8" square floral
- 13" x 21" rectangle cream tonal
- 4" x 14" strip navy print
- 7" x 9" rectangle blue petal print
- 4" x 14" strip dark purple print
- 6" x 7" rectangle light purple tonal
- 6" square yellow tonal
- 14" square green marble
- 8" x 9" rectangle dark green print

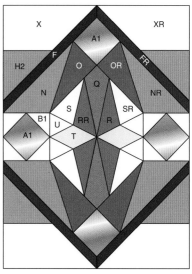

Starry Garden
16" x 22" Block

Cutting Instructions
Note: If you have previously cut all the pieces for the quilt, disregard these cutting instructions and go directly to Piecing the Block.

1. Prepare templates for F, N, O, Q, R, S, T, U and X pieces.

2. Refer to Cutting Chart on page 35 for cutting all pieces listed on templates for Starry Garden and below for best use of fabric.

3. Mark a dot at the seam-allowance corner on the wrong side of each Q, R and RR as marked on the patterns.

4. Cut four 3⅜" x 3⅜" A1 squares floral.

5. Cut four 2⅞" x 2⅞" squares cream tonal; cut each square in half on one diagonal to make eight B1 triangles.

6. Cut two 4⅞" x 4⅞" squares green marble; cut each square in half on one diagonal to make four H2 triangles.

Piecing the Block
1. Sew R to SR as shown in Figure 1; press seam toward SR. Repeat to make two each R-SR and RR-S units, again referring to Figure 1.

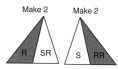

Make 2   Make 2

Figure 1

2. Sew an R-SR unit and an RR-S unit to opposite sides of Q as shown in Figure 2, stopping stitching at the marked corner dots of R, RR and Q; press seams toward R and RR. Repeat for two units.

Figure 2

3. Sew U to two adjacent edges of T as shown in Figure 3; press seams toward T. Repeat for two T-U units.

Figure 3

4. Sew a T-U unit to the RR-S edge of one pieced unit as shown in Figure 4, stopping stitching at the marked corner dot of RR; repeat for two units.

Figure 4

5. Join the pieced units as shown in Figure 5, stopping stitching at the marked corner dots of R and RR; press seams open between units.

Figure 5

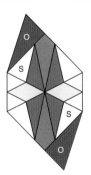

Figure 6

6. Sew O to opposite S edges of the pieced unit as shown in Figure 6; press seams toward O.

7. Sew A1 to the square end of each OR piece as shown in Figure 7; press seams toward OR.

Figure 7

8. Sew an A1-OR unit to the SR edges of the pieced unit to complete the center unit as shown in Figure 8; press seams toward A1-OR.

Figure 8

9. Sew B1 to each side of A1 as shown in Figure 9; press seams toward B1. Repeat for two A1-B1 units.

Figure 9

10. Sew N and NR to opposite sides of each A1-B1 unit as shown in Figure 10, stopping stitching at the marked corner dot on the N and NR pieces; press seams toward N and NR.

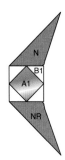

Figure 10

11. Sew the A1-B1 edge of the A1-B1-N units to the T-U edge of the pieced center unit, beginning and ending stitching at the marked corner dots on the N and NR pieces as shown in Figure 11.

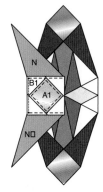

Figure 11

12. Sew the N and NR edges to the O and OR edges, beginning stitching at the marked corner dots on the N and NR pieces as shown in Figure 12; press seams toward A1-B1-N unit. Repeat on opposite T-U edge.

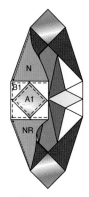

Figure 12

13. Sew F to the N edges and FR to the NR edges of the pieced unit as shown in Figure 13; press seams toward F and FR.

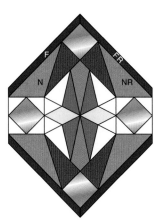

Figure 13

14. Sew H2 to X as shown in Figure 14; press seam toward H2. Repeat to make two each H2-X and H2-XR units, again referring to Figure 14.

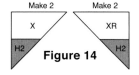

Figure 14

15. Sew the H2-X units to the F sides and the H2-XR units to the FR sides of the pieced unit to complete the block referring to the block drawing for positioning of units; press seams toward H2-X and H2-XR units. ∎

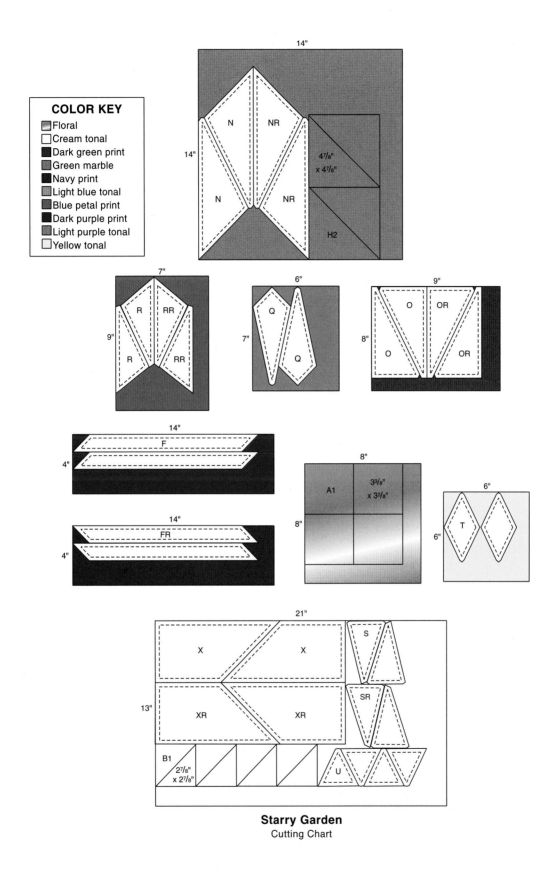

COLOR KEY
- Floral
- Cream tonal
- Dark green print
- Green marble
- Navy print
- Light blue tonal
- Blue petal print
- Dark purple print
- Light purple tonal
- Yellow tonal

Starry Garden
Cutting Chart

Completing the Center

Stitch sashing units to join your finished blocks into the quilt center.

PROJECT NOTE

It may be necessary to move seam allowances to one side or the other to reduce bulk when joining sashing units with other pieces and blocks.

FABRICS NEEDED

- ⅓ yard navy print
- ⅓ yard dark purple print
- ¾ yard floral
- 2 yards cream tonal

Cutting Instructions

Note: If you have previously cut all the pieces for the quilt, disregard these cutting instructions and go directly to the piecing instructions.

1. Cut one 4½" by fabric width strip each navy (G2) and dark purple (I2) prints; subcut strips into 18 each 1½" I2 and G2 strips.

2. Cut two 2½" x 21" strips each navy and dark purple prints. Prepare a template for H. Cut H and HR pieces from strips referring to Figure 1 and to the pattern for number to cut from each fabric.

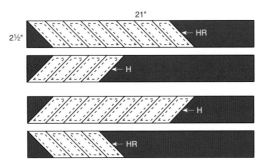

Figure 1

3. Cut one 5¼" by fabric width strip cream tonal; subcut strip into three 5¼" squares. Cut each square on both diagonals to make 12 P1 triangles.

4. Cut (13) 2⅞" by fabric width strips cream tonal; subcut strips into (176) 2⅞" squares. Cut each square in half on one diagonal to make 352 B1 triangles.

5. Cut two 2½" by fabric width strips cream tonal; subcut strips into two 28½" O1 strips and eight 2½" L1 squares.

6. Cut two 2½" by fabric width strips cream tonal; subcut strips into four each 8½" N1 and 10½" M1 strips.

7. Cut four 2½" by fabric width strips cream tonal for Q1 and R1 borders.

8. Cut seven 3⅜" by fabric width strips floral; subcut strips into (82) 3⅜" A1 squares.

Piecing the Sashing Units

1. Sew B1 to each side of A1 as shown in Figure 2; press seams toward B1. Repeat to make 82 A1-B1 units.

Figure 2

2. Sew a navy H to one short side and a dark purple HR to the remaining short side of eight P1 triangles as shown in Figure 3; press seams toward H and HR.

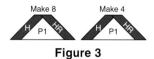

Figure 3

3. Repeat with navy HR and dark purple H pieces with four P1 triangles, again referring to Figure 3; press seams toward H and HR.

4. Sew B1 to the H and HR sides of each unit to complete eight sashing units and four reversed sashing units as shown in Figure 4; press seams toward B1.

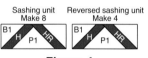 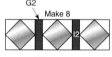

Figure 4   **Figure 5**

Completing the Center

1. Join three A1-B1 units with one each I2 and G2 strips as shown in Figure 5; press seams toward I2 and G2. Repeat to make eight strips.

2. Sew a strip to opposite sides of the Elongated Star block as shown in Figure 6; repeat with Tumbling Star, Four-Patch Star and Starry Hearts blocks. Press seams toward strips.

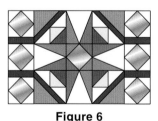 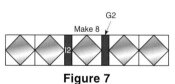

Figure 6   **Figure 7**

3. Join five A1-B1 units with one each I2 and G2 strips as shown in Figure 7; press seams toward I2 and G2. Repeat to make eight strips.

4. Sew a strip to the remaining sides of each of the four blocks as shown in Figure 8; press seams toward strips.

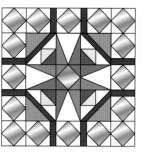

Figure 8

5. Sew the Star Reflections block between the Four-Patch Star and Tumbling Star blocks to make an end row as shown in Figure 9; press seams toward the Star Reflections block.

Figure 9

6. Sew the Starry Garden block between the Elongated Star and Starry Hearts blocks to make an end row, again referring to Figure 9; press seams toward the Starry Garden block.

7. Sew L1 to each end of four sashing units as shown in Figure 10; press seams toward L1.

Figure 10

COLOR KEY
- Floral
- Cream tonal
- Dark green print
- Green marble
- Navy print
- Light blue tonal
- Blue petal print
- Dark purple print
- Light purple tonal
- Yellow tonal

8. Sew a pieced strip to one side of each Tulips in the Corners and Nine-Patch Flowers blocks as shown in Figure 11; press seams toward pieced strips.

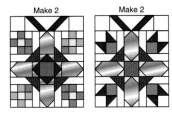

Figure 11

9. Join two A1-B1 units with one each I2 and G2 strip as shown in Figure 12; press seams toward I2 and G2. Repeat for two strips.

Figure 12

10. Join one each Tulips in the Corners and Nine-Patch Flowers blocks with one pieced strip as shown in Figure 13; press seams toward strips. Repeat.

Figure 13

11. Sew a block strip to opposite sides of the Basket Medallion block as shown in Figure 14; press seams toward the Basket Medallion block.

12. Sew O1 to opposite sides of the pieced section, again referring to Figure 14; press seams toward O1.

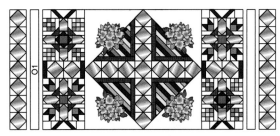

Figure 14

13. Join seven A1-B1 units to make a strip; press seams in one direction. Repeat for two strips.

14. Sew a strip to opposite sides of the pieced section to complete the center row, again referring to Figure 14; press seams toward O1.

15. Sew the center row between the two end rows referring to the Placement Diagram for positioning of rows; press seams toward the center row.

16. Join the Q1/R1 strips on short ends to make a long strip; press seams in one direction. Subcut strip into two 44½" Q1 strips and two 32½" R1 strips.

17. Join one Q1 and two N1 strips with two reversed sashing units to make a side strip as shown in Figure 15; press seams toward Q1 and N1. Repeat for two side strips.

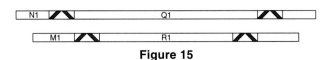

Figure 15

18. Join one R1 and two M1 strips with two sashing units to make an end strip, again referring to Figure 15; press seams toward R1 and M1. Repeat for two end strips.

19. Sew the side strips to opposite long sides of the pieced section and the end strips to the top and bottom referring to the Placement Diagram for positioning of strips; press seams toward strips to complete the center. ■

Adding the Pieced Border

This strip-pieced border adds a colorful frame to your pieced blocks and leaves you with only one more step to finish the quilt.

PROJECT NOTE

Refer to figure drawings showing placement of strips in the corners by color. Be careful when aligning seams for mitering corners.

FABRICS NEEDED

- ⅓ yard light blue tonal
- ⅓ yard navy print
- ⅓ yard light purple tonal
- ⅓ yard dark purple print
- ⅝ yard yellow tonal
- 1 yard dark green print

Cutting Instructions

Note: If you have previously cut all the pieces for the quilt, disregard these cutting instructions and go directly to the piecing instructions.

1. Cut seven 1½" by fabric width strips dark green print for Q2 and R2 borders.

2. Cut eight 2½" by fabric width strips dark green print for S2 and T2 borders.

3. Cut six 1½" by fabric width strips each light blue and light purple tonals and navy and dark purple prints.

4. Cut (12) 1½" by fabric width strips yellow tonal.

Adding the Borders

1. Join Q2/R2 strips on short ends to make a long strip; press seams in one direction. Subcut strip into two 76½" Q2 strips and two 66½" R2 strips.

2. Sew Q2 to opposite long sides of the completed center and R2 to the top and bottom; press seams toward strips.

3. Join one each light blue, navy, light purple and dark purple strips with two yellow strips to make a strip set as shown in Figure 1; press seams in one direction. Repeat to make six strip sets.

Figure 1

4. Cut the strip sets into (54) 4½" segments as shown in Figure 2.

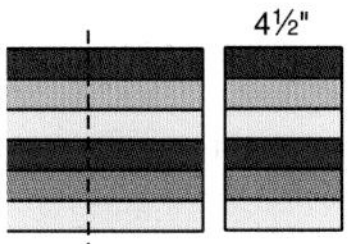

Figure 2

5. Join 13 segments and remove four strips from the yellow end to complete the top border as shown in Figure 3; press seams in one direction. This strip should begin with navy and end with light blue.

Remove

Figure 3

6. Join 14 segments, add the four strips removed in step 5 to the navy end and remove two strips from the yellow end to complete the right-side border as shown in Figure 4; press seams in one direction. This strip should begin with yellow and end with dark purple.

Add   Remove

Figure 4

7. Join 12 segments and add the two strips removed in step 6 to the navy end to complete the bottom border as shown in Figure 5; press seams in one direction. This strip should begin with light purple and end with yellow.

Add

Figure 5

8. Join 15 segments and remove four strips from the yellow end to complete the left-side border as shown in Figure 6; press seams in one direction. This strip should begin with navy and end with light blue.

Remove

Figure 6

9. Mark the center of each side of the bordered center section.

10. Center the top border strip right sides together with the top edge of the bordered center section with the navy strip on the left end and the light blue strip on the right end; place a pin at the center. Pin the remaining sections at 3"–4" intervals as shown in Figure 7. **Note:** *There should be four strip pieces extending beyond the O border at each end as shown in Figure 8.*

Figure 7

Figure 8

11. Stitch border strip to the center section, beginning and ending stitching ¼" from each end of the top edge, again referring to Figure 8; remove pins.

12. Repeat steps 10 and 11 with the remaining border strips, positioning strip colors as follows: yellow at top and dark purple at bottom on right-side edge, light purple at right and yellow at left on bottom edge, and navy at bottom and light blue at top on left-side edge. This arrangement continues the color order of the strips around the outside of the quilt.

13. Miter the border corners with strip seam lines matching at corners as shown in Figure 9.

Figure 9

Figure 10

14. Trim mitered corner seam to ¼" and press open as shown in Figure 10. Press border seams toward Q2 and R2 border.

15. Join the S2/T2 strips on short ends to make a long strip; press seams in one direction. Subcut strip into two 86½" S2 strips and two 78½" T2 strips.

16. Sew S2 to opposite long sides of the bordered center and T2 to the top and bottom; press seams toward strips to complete the pieced top. ■

COLOR KEY
- Floral
- Cream tonal
- Dark green print
- Green marble
- Navy print
- Light blue tonal
- Blue petal print
- Dark purple print
- Light purple tonal
- Yellow tonal

Completing Your Quilt

A wide floral border to hang over the edges of your bed adds the perfect finishing touch to your Dazzling Diamonds quilt.

PROJECT NOTE

Measure your finished quilt top from top to bottom through the center of the top to determine the actual size of your side border strips. Repeat from side to side through the center after sewing the side strips to determine the actual size of the top and bottom border strips.

PROJECT SPECIFICATIONS

Finished Quilt Size: 94" x 106"

FABRICS NEEDED

- ¾ yard dark green print
- 2¼ yards floral

OTHER MATERIALS

- 9½ yards backing fabric
- Batting 100" x 112"

Cutting Instructions

Note: If you have previously cut all the pieces for the quilt, disregard these cutting instructions and go directly to the Instructions.

1. Cut nine 8½" by fabric width strips floral for U2 and V2 borders.

2. Cut (10) 2¼" by fabric width strips dark green print for binding.

Instructions

1. Join the U2/V2 border strips on short ends with straight seams to make a long strip; press seams in one direction. Subcut strip into two 90½" U2 strips and two 94½" V2 strips.

2. Sew U2 to opposite long sides of the bordered center and V2 to the top and bottom; press seams toward strips to complete the top.

3. Mark the top for quilting, if desired.

4. Cut one fabric-width by 112" length and two 31½" x 112" lengths from backing fabric; remove selvage edges. Sew the fabric-width length between the two 31½"-wide lengths using a ½" seam allowance; press seams open to complete the quilt backing.

5. Sandwich the batting between the prepared backing piece and completed top; pin or baste to hold.

6. Hand- or machine-quilt as desired.

7. When quilting is complete, remove pins or basting. Trim batting and backing edges even with the quilted top.

8. Join the binding strips on short ends with diagonal seams to make a long strip; press seams in one direction. Press the strip in half along length with wrong sides together.

9. Sew binding to quilt edge with raw edges matching, mitering corners and overlapping beginning and end; turn to the back side. Hand- or machine-stitch in place to finish. ∎

Templates

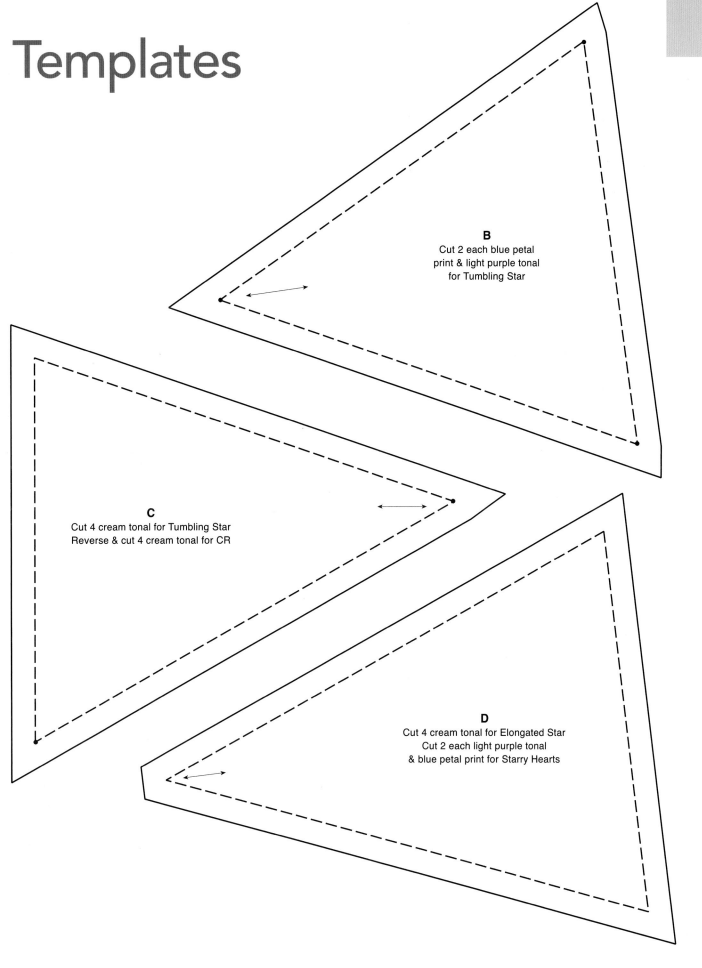

B
Cut 2 each blue petal
print & light purple tonal
for Tumbling Star

C
Cut 4 cream tonal for Tumbling Star
Reverse & cut 4 cream tonal for CR

D
Cut 4 cream tonal for Elongated Star
Cut 2 each light purple tonal
& blue petal print for Starry Hearts

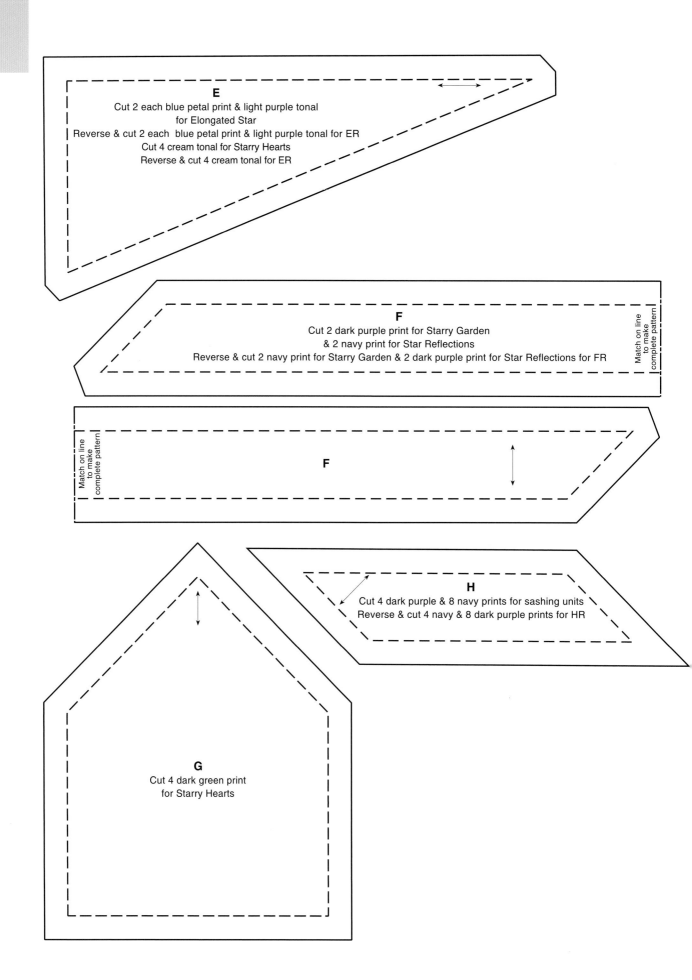

E

Cut 2 each blue petal print & light purple tonal
for Elongated Star
Reverse & cut 2 each blue petal print & light purple tonal for ER
Cut 4 cream tonal for Starry Hearts
Reverse & cut 4 cream tonal for ER

F

Cut 2 dark purple print for Starry Garden
& 2 navy print for Star Reflections
Reverse & cut 2 navy print for Starry Garden & 2 dark purple print for Star Reflections for FR

Match on line
to make
complete pattern

F

Match on line
to make
complete pattern

H

Cut 4 dark purple & 8 navy prints for sashing units
Reverse & cut 4 navy & 8 dark purple prints for HR

G
Cut 4 dark green print
for Starry Hearts

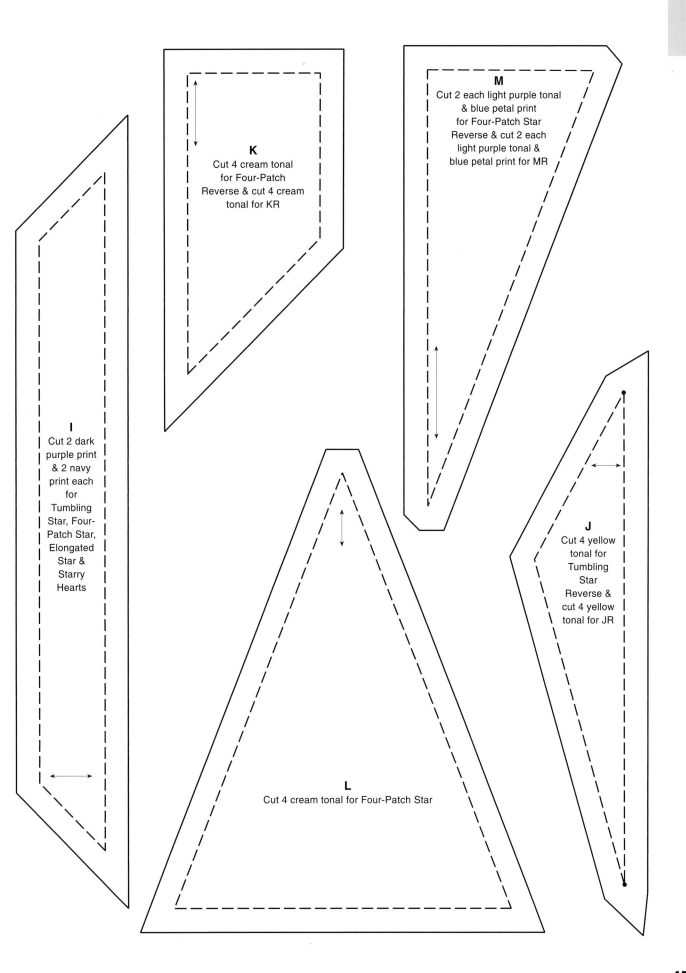

K
Cut 4 cream tonal
for Four-Patch
Reverse & cut 4 cream
tonal for KR

M
Cut 2 each light purple tonal
& blue petal print
for Four-Patch Star
Reverse & cut 2 each
light purple tonal &
blue petal print for MR

I
Cut 2 dark
purple print
& 2 navy
print each
for
Tumbling
Star, Four-
Patch Star,
Elongated
Star &
Starry
Hearts

J
Cut 4 yellow
tonal for
Tumbling
Star
Reverse &
cut 4 yellow
tonal for JR

L
Cut 4 cream tonal for Four-Patch Star

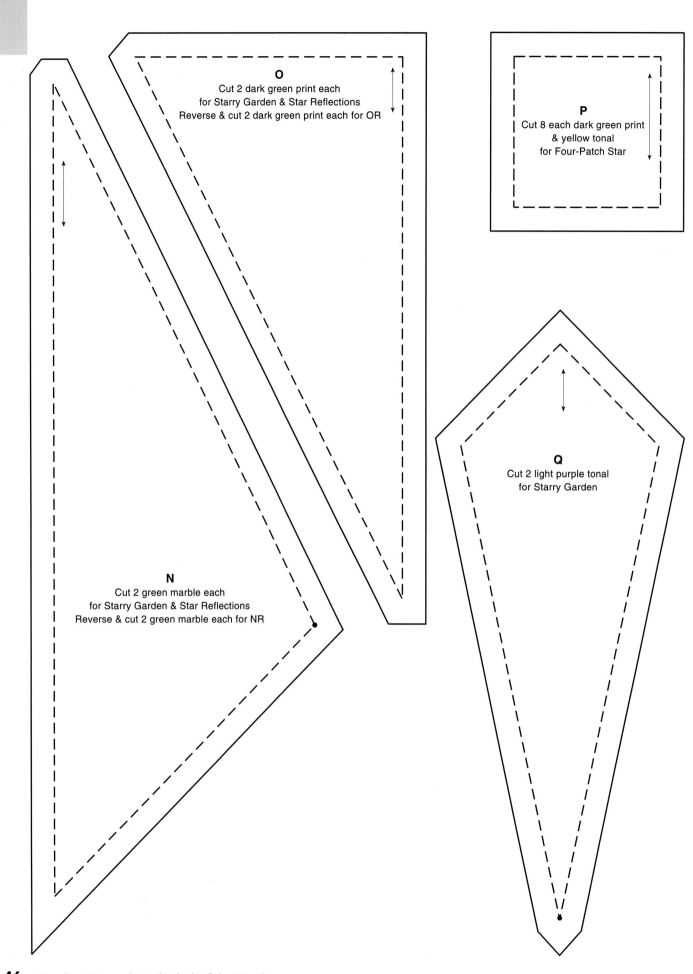

O
Cut 2 dark green print each
for Starry Garden & Star Reflections
Reverse & cut 2 dark green print each for OR

P
Cut 8 each dark green print
& yellow tonal
for Four-Patch Star

Q
Cut 2 light purple tonal
for Starry Garden

N
Cut 2 green marble each
for Starry Garden & Star Reflections
Reverse & cut 2 green marble each for NR

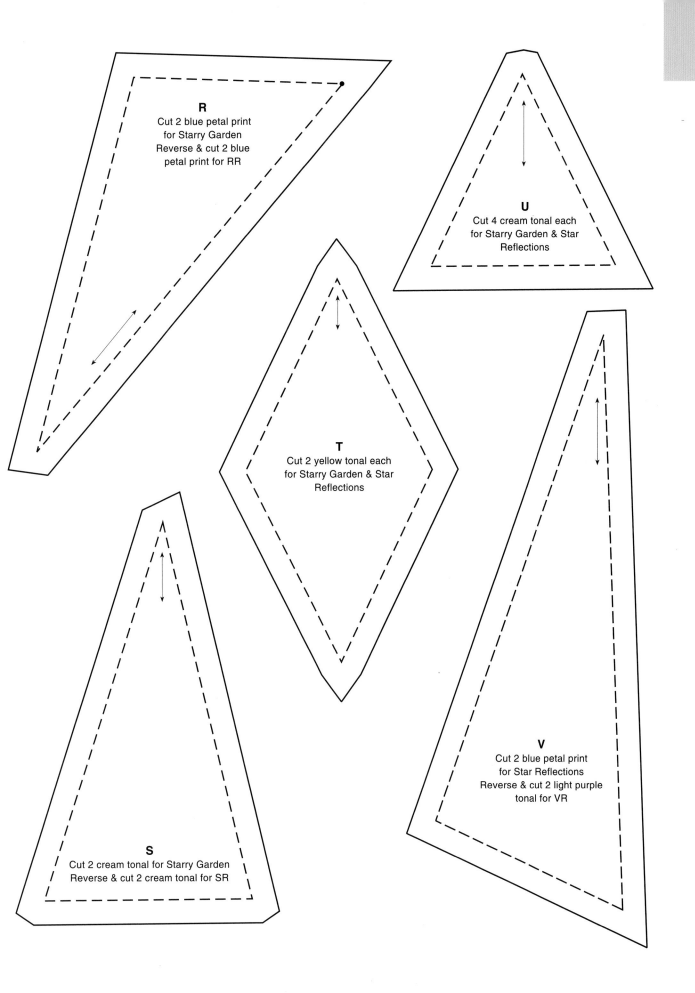

R
Cut 2 blue petal print
for Starry Garden
Reverse & cut 2 blue
petal print for RR

U
Cut 4 cream tonal each
for Starry Garden & Star
Reflections

T
Cut 2 yellow tonal each
for Starry Garden & Star
Reflections

S
Cut 2 cream tonal for Starry Garden
Reverse & cut 2 cream tonal for SR

V
Cut 2 blue petal print
for Star Reflections
Reverse & cut 2 light purple
tonal for VR

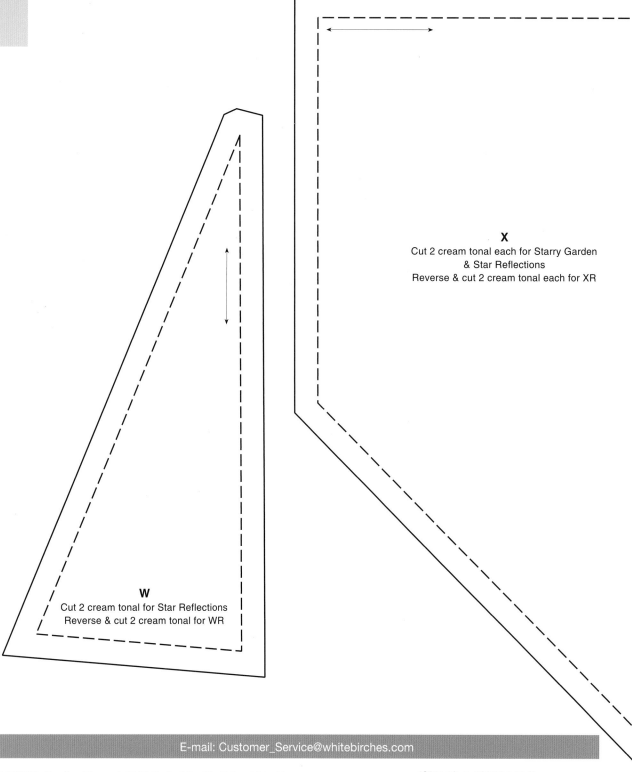

X
Cut 2 cream tonal each for Starry Garden
& Star Reflections
Reverse & cut 2 cream tonal each for XR

W
Cut 2 cream tonal for Star Reflections
Reverse & cut 2 cream tonal for WR

E-mail: Customer_Service@whitebirches.com

HOUSE of WHITE BIRCHES
PUBLISHERS SINCE 1947

Dazzling Diamonds Quilt Block of the Month is published by House of White Birches, 306 East Parr Road, Berne, IN 46711, telephone (260) 589-4000. Printed in USA. Copyright © 2006 House of White Birches.

RETAIL STORES: If you would like to carry this pattern book or any other House of White Birches publications, call the Wholesale Department at Annie's Attic to set up a direct account: (903) 636-4303. Also, request a complete listing of publications available from House of White Birches.

ISBN-10: 1-59217-144-3
ISBN-13: 978-1-59217-144-6
1 2 3 4 5 6 7 8 9

STAFF
Editors: Jeanne Stauffer, Sandra L. Hatch
Associate Editor: Dianne Schmidt
Technical Artist: Connie Rand
Copy Supervisor: Michelle Beck
Copy Editors: Sue Harvey, Nicki Lehman, Judy Weatherford
Graphic Arts Supervisor: Ronda Bechinski

Graphic Artists: Debby Keel, Edith Teegarden
Art Director: Brad Snow
Assistant Art Director: Nick Pierce
Photography: Tammy Christian, Don Clark, Matthew Owen, Jackie Schaffel
Photo Stylists: Tammy Nussbaum, Tammy M. Smith

Every effort has been made to ensure that the instructions in this pattern book are complete and accurate. We cannot, however, take responsibility for human error, typographical mistakes or variations in individual work.

The quilt was professionally machine-quilted by Dianne Hodgkins. Fabrics supplied by RJR Fabrics. Batting supplied by Fairfield Processing. Piecing and quilting thread supplied by Coats.